THE ELEVATOR PITCH OF YOU

USE NEUROSCIENCE TO CRAFT A UNIQUE AND POWERFUL PERSONAL BRAND STATEMENT FOR USE IN YOUR RESUME, CV, AND LINKEDIN

By

DAVID C WINEGAR

Copyright © 2017

www.createmybrand.us

INTRODUCTION

The Elevator Pitch of You powerfully combines a book and an online tool to help you create a personal brand statement that influences how people perceive you. Its purpose is to evoke positive emotions, thoughts, and images in people, setting you apart from the competition.

Just as a well-written elevator pitch sells a start-up to investors, your well-crafted brand statement will help you win the hearts and minds of those important to your success.

How does it work? The book takes you through the latest neuroscience research into how your brain processes information and shows you how to use that to build a better personal brand statement. You find out how to use the same techniques that modern consumer brand managers use to influence people's perceptions and buying behavior. It is easier than you think. This book offers unique insight that will change forever how you answer the question of who you are and how others perceive you.

2

You get exclusive access to our online brand survey that creates a step-by-step personal workbook for developing your brand statement. The heavy work has already been done to provide you with insight and direction to build your brand statement with ease. The book provides plenty of examples for inspiration, and word-by-word takes you through how to build your own statement from your survey results.

You can use your statement:

1. In job interviews, to help you confidently answer the question: "Tell us about yourself?"

2. On your resumé or CV, to give a clear picture of what sets you apart from the competition.

3. As a killer LinkedIn profile summary.

4. As a personal statement for your business.

5. For leaders and team managers who want their teams to understand who they are and how to work better with them.

Start your personal brand journey today.

ONLINE BRAND TOOL ACCESS

To access the online companion tool for this book please visit http://createmybrand.us and follow the link.

TAKE MY VIDEO COURSE

Join my Udemy video course and get more insight into personal branding and additional help with creating your own brand. Use the link below and save big off the $29.99 price of the course. Just $9.99 for lifetime access with 100% money back guarantee. Also, makes a great gift for the recent graduate or new job seeker.

https://www.udemy.com/neuroscience-of-personal-branding/?couponCode=EPOYBOOK

JOIN ME ONLINE

Need help with your statement? Want to get some feedback? Join our Facebook group for the readers of this book.

http://bit.ly/EPYBook

GET MY NEW BOOK BRAINSIGHTS

If this book has peaked your interest in neuroscience, I invite you to read my latest release, *Brainsights*. Released in December of 2018, Brainsights is a review of more than 240 original neuroscience research studies. I break down the science into everyday language and show you how to put the research to work to live, love and lead a better life.

Available worldwide on your favorite book platform in print and eBook (just type "Brainsights" into the book search). Vist my Amazon author page to learn more:

https://www.amazon.com/David-C-Winegar/e/B076ZBW2M4

ABOUT THE AUTHOR:

David C Winegar is an author, trainer, coach, speaker, and applied neuroscience advocate who travels the world helping organizations and individuals to achieve more through a better understanding of human behavior. His work has taken him to four continents, coaching 1 000s of people from over 70 countries.

Before getting his MBA in organizational behavior and eBusiness from the University of Pittsburgh, he had a diverse work background including; working at the Smithsonian Institution's American History Museum, at the National Archives of the United States of America as a top-secret records declassification expert, and an international teacher of history and geography in Helsinki, Finland.

Since receiving his MBA in 1995, he has been in no less than six tech start-up companies, 3 in the US and 3 in Finland, including a forerunner to Twitter and one of the first mobile email services.

For the last 11 years, he has been running his organizational development and coaching consulting firm, Absolute-North Ltd., which uses the latest psychological and neuroscience research to develop people. He has developed an experiential learning method called Artificial Experience Building, which uses neuroscience-backed research to better commit learning to long-term memory.

David's work has been in a broad spectrum of industries, everything from mobile gaming, and SAS companies, to industrial equipment, shipping, and machinery.

He lives in Helsinki, Finland, with his wife Satu, son Tomas, and his French Briard dog Leo.

Table of Contents

Quantity Ordering Information:

Quantity sales. Special discounts are available on quantity purchases by corporations, associations, and others. For details, contact the publisher at the address above.

WHAT IS AN ELEVATOR PITCH?

With all the start-up successes generated from the internet and mobile companies in the last 25 years, most of you have likely already heard of the term "elevator pitch." But what exactly is it?

An elevator pitch is a 60- to 90-second proposal that outlines what you are selling and why someone should buy it. The urban myth is that the term came from Hollywood and was what screenwriters used to pitch new movie and TV ideas, expressing their blockbuster ideas concisely in the time it took to go from the ground floor to the penthouse office. However, the actual source of the term "elevator pitch" is a little less glamorous. It was likely first used by the Otis Elevator company to demonstrate the system that stopped an elevator from plummeting to the earth if the rope broke.

What, then, is a personal elevator pitch? It is similar idea to a business elevator pitch, but this time the idea is you.

Let's explore more and start on the path to creating your unique brand statement and the "Elevator Pitch of You."

WHAT IS A BRAND?

A BRIEF HISTORY OF BRANDS

Before we get started on building your brand and formulating the elevator pitch of you, let's briefly explore the history of brands and how they developed over the centuries.

The modern word "brand" is derived from the Norse word "brandr" and can be traced back to 950 AD and literally meant to burn. It was not until the 1500s that the meaning changed from to burn (like a torch) to burn into, to mark ownership – think cattle. Individual cattle owners would each have their unique mark on the animals to establish proof of ownership if lost, stolen, or mixed with other animals. Each "brand" had to be simple, unique, and easy to identify quickly.

The first brand-related legislation dates back to 1266, when King Henry II of England required that all bakers use a distinctive mark for the bread they made and sold.

The rise of mass production and global shipping in the early 1800s resulted in a need to identify goods in a similarly quick and easy way. Producers burned their brands, or logos, into crates and barrels of goods. Over time, brands moved from just being a mark of ownership to also being a mark of quality. However, it was not until 1870 that it became possible to register a brand (or trademark) to prevent competitors from creating products that would be too similar to other products, which could be confusing to the consumer.

Fast forward another few decades. the first comprehensive trademark system was passed into law in France in 1857. Also in 1857, England enacted the Trade Marks Registration Act protecting a "device, mark, or name of an individual or firm."

The oldest known registered trademark is the logo of the brewing company Bass. Their distinctive red logo with script text which can still be found today. The oldest registered trademark in the US is from rope manufacturer Samson Rope Technologies, formerly known as J.P. Tolman Company.

With the invention of the radio and television manufacturers created new ways to generate demand for products. In 1928, Sigmund Freud's nephew, Edward L. Bernays, published a book called *Propaganda*. The book argued that by associating products with ideas, companies could convince large numbers of people to change their behavior and buy their products. The book was widely popular and helped to form the basis of modern advertising. It is ironic that the word "propaganda" today is seen as cynical and manipulative. For the readers of the early 1920s, propaganda was seen as necessary to sustain economic growth.

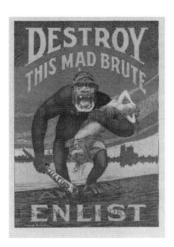

World War I was the first time propaganda techniques were systematically used by governments to target and alter public perceptions of the war. The British and Americans used propaganda to demonize the Germans and paint them as an evil menace. One of the most poignant forms of propaganda used was atrocity propaganda which embellished the most violent acts committed by the Germans to "mold" public opinion against them. They used media to depict the Germans as inhumane savages. Government-led propaganda was efficient and showed the power of how media can manipulate hearts and minds.

In the 1950s and 60s researchers like Harvey Leibenstein (*Bandwagon, snob and Veblen effects in the theory of consumer*

18

demand) and Vance Packard (*The Hidden Persuaders*) formulated the modern ideas around which successful bands are built. Ideas that connected what we buy with who we are. A brand came to signify the desired lifestyle and became a social badge. Ralph Lauren today is an excellent example of a brand that has used this concept extensively, using imagery to invoke a feeling and a lifestyle that people aspire.

CONNECTING COMPANY BRANDS TO PERSONAL BRANDS

Now that we have a basic understanding of brands, how do we apply that knowledge to the brand that is you? Many of the earliest company brands were in fact individuals who named the company after themselves. People guaranteed the quality of their products

individually and put their name and face to them. A great example is the "Jimmy Branch Company" of Panama City, Florida. In the 1950s, a small-town businessman named Jimmy Branch opened many businesses all with his name on them. He had Jimmy's Drive-In, Jimmy's Car Wash, and 14 restaurants in total – all with his name on them. Jimmy understood the power of personal branding.

Take it up in scale and you also find a lot of companies named after the founders, Ford, Rockefeller, Sears & Roebuck, J.C. Penney, Daimler-Benz, even Adidas is an abbreviation of the founder's name, Adolf Dassler (Adi is short for Adolf).

We think of personal branding as a new concept but, as we have seen, the history of branding is filled with examples of personal brands.

THE EVOLUTION OF THE CONCEPT OF A BRAND

As we move into the information age, brands evolved from company and products to individuals themselves being the brand. The person becomes the engine that forms impressions in the public's mind about the lifestyle they aspire to. Today, hundreds

20

of celebrities use their name and image to sell a countless number of products not made by them.

Donald Trump, Kayne West, Rihanna, The Kardashian clan, Taylor Swift, the list goes on and on. Cumulatively the world's 100 top-earning celebrities earned $5.15 billion between June 2016 and June 2017 (Forbes Jun 12, 2017). The brand of 'me' has become the engine that sells people their dreams.

BUT I'M NOT A CELEBRITY. WHY DO I NEED A BRAND?

You don't have to be a multi-platinum record selling artist, or President of the United States to need a brand. What does branding do? It helps us stand out from the crowd.

A recent Time.com article on the resumé trends for 2018 declares the objective statement dead.

"Objective statements on your resume are a thing of the past .... Use a summary statement instead, which is basically just an elevator pitch for why you're the best person for this job."

Creating a well-formulated and managed brand statement can stimulate those areas of the brain responsible for memories, emotions, and impressions. Isn't this the key to connecting with others?

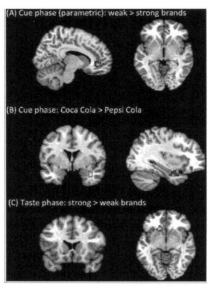

An influential study published in 2013 by Simone Kühn and Jürgen Gallinat (*Does Taste Matter? How Anticipation of Cola Brands Influences Gustatory Processing in the Brain*) found that when people knew they were drinking Coca-Cola, different parts of their brains lit up in the fMRI machines than those that were not told what they were drinking. The left ventral striatum had a much stronger activation when participants were told they were drinking Coca-Cola.

In another study published in 2008 (*Prefrontal cortex damage abolishes brand-cued changes in cola preference.* Koenigs M. & Tranel D.) it was found that persons with damage to their ventromedial prefrontal cortex (VMOC), that area of our brains important for emotion, did not have this preference bias for a cola triggered by the brand alone.

What this shows is how powerful branding can be. Good branding can trigger the release of chemicals in our brain that give us positive emotions.

Using similar product marketing techniques, you have the possibility to also develop powerful emotional responses to your name and the brand you have created around yourself.

SAMENESS SUCKS

The brilliant marketing and management guru, Gary Hamel, is credited with the phrase "sameness sucks." In a bland world where every product looks the same, every cup of coffee, car, pair of jeans, and shoes, understanding how to stand out is the only thing that matters.

This is also true of people. When it comes to job applications. Nowadays, hundreds, if not thousands, of people apply for one single vacant position. We think those looking through the applications are seeking the best candidate for the position. But in the first couple of rounds of evaluation, it is not about finding the best candidate – it is about getting rid of the garbage and narrowing the field down to the 10 who are potential interview material. The trick to getting to the interview round is to stand out and be memorable.

If you think everyone has put in the time to properly brand themselves, this is not true. Most don't spend the time, or have the knowledge, to create a statement and therefore just skip it and put something at the top of their resumé that is the desperate equivalent of "hire me, I need a job."

How do you stand out? What makes you better than 50 other people with the same education and experience as you have? The only way to set yourself apart from the competition is through personal branding. This includes the "elevator pitch of you" that, in less than 60 seconds, convinces others you are worth their time and attention.

Let me tell a short story from my experience of how tough it is in the job market to get noticed. My wife used to work for a company that needed to fill a position within the organization. They placed an ad in the local newspaper, a paper with a readership of about 100 000. Within a matter of days, they had applications from hundreds of job seekers. The number was so overwhelming that those responsible complained; "How can we possibly read through all the applications?" The boss of the department just smiled, took a handful of job applications, and threw them in the trashcan as everyone looked on. Shocked, one person spoke up and said, "What are you doing?"

His reply? "Those people had bad luck. We don't want anyone in our company with bad luck, do we?"

This is, of course, an extreme example and one that is impossible to fight against. But what you can fight against is the rapid assessment and dismissal of your application from the pool by clearly standing out.

THE IMPORTANCE OF A BRAND STATEMENT

Personal branding is the single most important way to stand out. A brand statement is a promise. It communicates a pledge of your unique value and what you bring, or will bring, to the organization. It also, maybe more importantly, communicates how you will make a positive impact on the people you will work. Organizational success is tightly tied to teams and their ability to work better together.

Google's "Project Aristotle" was a project undertook in 2012 to investigate what makes some teams successful while others fail. The findings surprised all in the project. It was not about individual or collective intelligence, or diversity. What separated high-performing teams from dysfunctional teams was how members of the team treated one another. High-performing teams understand better each other and give more support to one another. They care about including everyone and actively make sure that team members are included and listened to. They have a strong sense of psychological safety.

Communicating your ability to work well within a team and be a person that is able to support others in developing their full potential, becomes essential to learn how to project.

Let's look at where and how you can use your branding statement and what it can do to position you better in the minds of those you want to influence.

UNDERSTANDING THE BRAIN AND HOW IT PROCESSES INFORMATION

Neuroscientist now are confident in their understanding of the functional areas of the brain. The rapid advancement in this field has come from being able to put humans into a fMRI machine and watch, in real-time, what areas of the brain are being stimulated.

The fMRI machine was invented in 1990 by Bell Laboratories and was a giant leap forward in helping us to understand how the brain processes information. fMRI stands for 'functional magnetic resonance imaging' and can measure brain activity in real time. This can provide a visual representation of which parts of the brain are being triggered as people undergo tasks, listen, and view information.

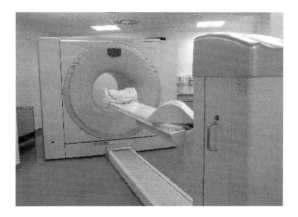

Neuroscience is the science that has come out of the study of the nervous system and seeks to understand the biological basis of behavior.

My first encounter with the power of the fMRI machine came in 2012 when I by chance came across a researcher from Israel, Eric Feingold of Feingold Technologies. Feingold had developed an algorithm that could predict the effectiveness of a sales message by examining only the tone of voice of a person presenting.

The way the algorithm was developed was by putting subjects into fMRI machines and then testing different messages and recording which parts of the brain lit up. They sampled a million messages and found that the resulting algorithm was an accurate predictor of successful sales communication. It was a fascinating example of the power of neuroscience and how it could be applied to help people be more successful.

Influential Israeli-American psychologist Daniel Kahneman (*Thinking Fast and Slow, 2011*) showed how marketers could use brain research to speak directly to the subconscious and influence buying decisions.

Understanding how the brain works and how it has evolved is essential to understanding how to influence and connect better with people. The goal of your brand statement should be to trigger the right areas of the subconscious to influence positively the perception people have of you.

THE PARTS OF THE BRAIN

We can divide the brain into roughly two systems, which Kahneman termed simply as system 1 and system 2.

The System 1 Brain

System 1 is our automatic and nonconscious brain and is always on to protect us from perceived threats. It is often referred to as the "lizard brain" or "old brain" because it is that brain that has evolved from our most primitive ancestors. It is the *fast decision maker*.

System 1 is responsible for basic functions such as our heartbeat, breathing, and walking. Even talking and language are part of our system 1 lizard brains. Just imagine if you had to spend the time to process the act of taking a single step or saying a single word and you understand that these automatic brain functions are necessary.

The place where we get in trouble with our system 1 brains is in making near instantaneous assessments of people and situations based on incomplete information. In less than .07 of a second the system 1 brain determines threat or no threat.

Many of us refer to this feeling as our "gut feeling" and neuroscience has shown that this is something that is real. We have a strong neural connection between our guts and our brain and this connection influences our emotions.

We relied on our gut feelings in the past to help protect us from predators and those that would seek to do us harm. Imagine being on the savannah of Africa and a person or wild animal running full speed towards you. You didn't have time to use your system 2 logical brain to evaluate the danger this situation presented to you. Your S1 brain made it for you and tended to always error on the side of caution.

The implications of this near-instantaneous gut feeling decisions in the modern world is profound. It is impossible to get all the relevant information about a person in the modern-day world in .07 seconds. We inevitably get it wrong and end up judging a person as a threat when in fact we have just misread the signals.

As an example, think of how to use your body language to signal to your neighbors you are not a threat. When you see them from afar, you nod your head and raise your eyebrows, which is a universal signal you will not harm them. Even the common handshake is a gesture for showing you are not carrying a weapon, and the drink toast, showing that the wine has not been poisoned.

When you are writing your brand statement, you want to be sure you do the literary equivalent of these "I'm not a threat" signals. You want to be sure you are not saying something that can be interpreted as dangerous. It may sound obvious, but it is harder than you think.

Try this exercise. Read the following sentences aloud with different tones. Grab a partner and try it with them for the full effect.

> I didn't say she loved me.
> I **DIDN'T** say she loved me.
> I didn't **SAY** she loved me.
> I didn't say **SHE** loved me.
> I didn't say she **LOVED** me.
> I didn't say she loved **ME**.

You can take anything that people write and turn it around to something negative just by adding tone. Tone is why we get in so much trouble with our written digital communications. We look at emojis as just a way of adding fun to a message, but their purpose is much more. Emojis can help us communicate tone to people rather than leaving it to the reader to blindly determine our tone and intent.

In a groundbreaking 2013 study by Hannah Gacey and Jim Gallo, they asked 152 business professionals to read an email message with and without smiley emoticons. Here are examples:

> *I can't make the meeting you scheduled because it conflicts with my staff meeting. Email me and let me know what I missed.*
>
> vs.
>
> *I can't make the meeting you scheduled because it conflicts with my staff meeting. Email me and let me know what I missed. :-)*

When questioned about what they read, the results showed that the message with the emoticon reduced significantly the negative tone of the message.

I am not suggesting that you fill your brand statement with emoticons, but you should think carefully about the tone you are projecting. Try reading it with different tones and see how it sounds. Remember that if you are unfortunate and end up having your statement read by a person having a bad day, they are likely to read negative tone into it. What you want is a statement that is impossible to be interpreted as negative. Ideally, you would like your statement to change their mood and put that smiley face on their face.

Another study – this one by neuroscientist Dr. Paul Zak and digital and engagement strategy director Uwe Gurshow of Innocean – looked at people's emotional connections to brands to see if they could rival the emotional connection we have to people. Surprisingly they found that it was possible for a person to have a higher emotional response to a brand than to a loved one in their lives. Importantly, they found that the connection was only stronger when tied to a story. For example, one subject had a higher emotional response to a watch brand he loved than to his girlfriend. When investigating deeper why this was the case it was revealed that the watch was given to him by a beloved grandfather.

When considering how to present yourself, always keep the power of the story in mind. Stories resonate with our evolved brains and make social interactions rewarding. Your goal should be to develop an engaging story of who you are and what you can do.

THE SYSTEM 2 BRAIN

The System 2 brain is our slow-thinking brain. It is responsible for the cognitive functions of our brain, solving equations and thinking logically about things. It takes time to evaluate information and makes decisions based on the information provided. But it is painful work for us humans.

One significant truth about human beings is that our brains constantly look for shortcuts. We don't like to think long and hard about things and are more comfortable relying on our system 1 lizard brains to do the work for us.

Let me demonstrate how your brain works. Take this math problem:

$$2\left[3(4+7) - 2(6-3)\right]$$

Most of us can solve this equation without too much difficulty which means our brains did not have to work too hard or use too much energy.

But if we take a more involved thought problem, you start to see how lazy our brains are.

Question: You are running a race with 3 people. If you pass the second to the last person, what place are you in? First? Second? Or third?

Many of us find this word problem frustrating. Our bodies will even react by our heart rate going up and our muscles tensing. Why? Because our brains are wired to look for shortcuts. In pre-historic times, we spent most of our days desperately trying to find enough calories to survive. When our bodies are starved of energy, we look for ways to conserve by limiting functions that are unnecessary. Our brains have evolved to be "lazy" and look for the shortest possible routes. Therefore, we prefer to just take the snap judgment of our system 1 lizard brain, our "gut feeling", and go with that.

37

When writing your brand statement, it is wise to remember the brains preference for the easy solution. Don't make people work to hard to understand who you are, make it simple for them to see you as a competent and kind person.

What is even more surprising from the research is even when we get our system 2 brain involved in thinking logically, it prefers to rely on the information it received from the system 1 lizard brain. What happens is the lizard brain makes a quick decision, and then the logical brain tries to connect facts to the "feeling" it gets to justify it was right.

I know some of you are getting stressed about the answer to the previous word problem. Your "lazy" brain is making you feel bad not having the answer, so I will give you the answer – you are in second place. Can you feel first the stress and annoyance, and then the relief when you get the easy answer? This is how your brain shows you it dislikes expending energy on things it deems unnecessary.

I have coached many salespeople over the years, and this is one of the key points I try to get them to understand. It is not about

38

telling all the logical reasons about why someone should buy your product or service. It is about first getting the system 1 lizard brain to see you as someone that will help and not hurt them. That is how the buying decision is made; it is only after they have system 1 lizard brain approval that they move to the logical brain to justify why they want to buy from you.

If we think of the impact you want to make with your brand statement, the most essential element is to appease the system 1 lizard brain. The mistake people make in their statements on LinkedIn and on their resumes and CVs is listing just facts about what they have accomplished. They think people are logical and that they want to hear what they can do. But it is very important to always remember this quote from USC Professor of Neuroscience Antonio Damasio:

> "We are not thinking machines. We are feeling machines that think."

Focus your brand on the feeling part first and then add the logical to support the feeling you created.

North Carolina State University researcher Roger Myer and Purdue University researcher David Shoorman found that you need to score well on integrity and honesty in order to positively connect with people. The four qualities necessary to score high are the 4Cs:

1. **Capability**: I believe you have the appropriate knowledge and skills (i.e. you possess competence, knowledge and ability that make me trust you).

2. **Caring**: I believe you are on my side (i.e. you display empathy, warmth and caring about my wants and needs).

3. **Candor**: I believe you will act with honesty and integrity (i.e. you will follow through on your promises and not deceive me).

4. **Consistency**: I believe you will act in a predictable and reliable manner (i.e. you behave in a dependable manner that minimizes surprises).

When creating your brand statement, keep in mind these 4Cs and be sure you are hitting on as many of them as you can.

40

People when reading your statement should be able to answer these two simple questions:

Why would anyone want to spend every day working with you?

How are you going to help the company – and more importantly me – to be more successful?

Friendliness and competence in balance – this is the key. Accomplish that in your statement and you will set yourself apart from the crowd.

TYPES OF PERSONAL BRAND STATEMENTS

There are two types of brand statements, ones for potential employers and ones for working better in your current organization. Although statements share common elements – such as how you would prefer to be perceived and what you value – the tone and the focus is different.

It is also important to recognize that your position within your organization will impact how you write your statement. For example, if you are responsible for managing others, your statement will be different from a team or matrix project leader.

Let's look at some examples to help give you a clearer picture and some inspiration.

INSPIRATIONAL BRAND STATEMENTS

I want to start by showing you a few brand statements from individuals who have made a name for themselves. The idea is to provide you with some inspiration and show you how the mix of warmth and competency can be effective in the real world.

The first example I want to show you is from Madeleine Albright. Former US Secretary of State and US Ambassador to the United Nations, she could speak only of her impressive political achievements and most would be satisfied. But Albright also understands the importance of warmth when it comes to connecting with people. Let's look at her Twitter profile.

Twitter is a tough place to get your branding just right due to the limit on the number of characters allowed. But her profile is a shining example of what can be accomplished.

Her bio reads:

> Grateful American, Czech immigrant, mother & grandmother, fmr SecState, passionate democrat, author, prof, bizwoman, pin collector & occasional drummer.

Let's break down her statement so you can see the elements of warmth and competence she has included.

First, the warmth elements. Being grateful to be an American is a statement meant to open our eyes to her views on what it means to be an American. As an immigrant, she found all the

43

opportunities to reach the highest level of success in the United States, something that would have been impossible in the communist-controlled Czechoslovakia of the post WWII era.

Next, she focuses us on the fact she is a mother and grandmother. Again, she is humanizing herself. We all have mothers and grandmothers and can relate to her and demonstrates to us the importance of family, a quality that many place importance on.

Now it is time for her to tell us about her competencies. She lists that she is a former US Secretary of State, author, professor, and business woman. These all tell us a lot about who she is and her abilities. Not to mention it makes us want to learn more about her and what she has done, something we all would like to motivate people to do with our own statements.

She throws in a quirky little side note within those accomplishments, "passionate democrat," meant to humanize herself. Political affiliations are risky for you to include in your statement, unless you are looking to work in for an organization that is strongly politically affiliated. For Madeleine, is a part of who she is and her political life so it's not a problem.

44

Finally, she focuses us back on her warmth in a clever way. She mentions she is a pin collector and an occasional drummer. Wow! Sorry, but this just blows me away. Here is one of the most accomplished women in modern politics and she is using the limited character space on her Twitter profile to tell us these two ostensibly innocent facts. But think about it... Doesn't it make her so much more approachable? Can you picture her with a hat full of pins at some pin collector event? Or behind the kit knocking out a killer backbeat? I must admit that I struggled with that image, but it is something that intrigued me. Being a drummer myself it was something that hit me close to the heart.

It is an amazing example of the power of warmth and competency in balance.

Next is author and Ted Talk phenomenon Simon Sinek. Sinek is a bestselling author and key note speaker. He talks common sense leadership and ideas that motivate and inspire people to work better together.

In LinkedIn, his profile reads as follows:

> I imagine a world where almost everyone wakes up inspired to go to work, feels trusted and valued during the day, then returns home feeling fulfilled, like they have contributed to something greater than themselves. My team and I believe in this bright future and our ability to build it together.

Let's break down his statement and see why it is a good example of a brand statement.

Firstly, Sinek uses one of the most powerful words in sales, "imagine." When you ask people to imagine something you are not asking them to commit to buy or to give anything, you are only asking them to think about what it is you are saying. Here he is asking us to think about a world where we are inspired to go to work, where we feel trusted and valued. Powerful stuff.

He goes on to speak about returning home feeling fulfilled in having accomplished something greater. Again, isn't this what we all would like out of our jobs? Sinek is setting himself up as the one that can help us all to understand how to accomplish this.

Lastly, he connects us to his team. He is not in this alone, right? It takes others to execute on such a grand vision and he remembers to include them.

Another good example of a compelling brand statement comes from Jenny Blake. Blake is woman from New York who has built a successful blog, and is an author, speaker and coach. She is known for helping others "Wake up, live big, and love the Journey."

Let's look at her branding statement from the first page of her website at pivotmethod.com:

> I'm an author, speaker, career coach and business strategist living in New York City. I love helping awesome people like you organize your brain, move beyond burnout and build a sustainable career you love.

> I'm fascinated by strategies for navigating change in our rapidly-evolving economy, and I geek out exploring and creating systems at the intersection of mind, body and business. I live for helping smart, talented, optimistic people like you embrace chaos, fear, insecurity and uncertainty as doorways of opportunity.

After a quick overview of what she does, Blake moves on to what drives her and why it should matter to us. She loves helping "awesome" people like us to organize our brains and move ourselves and careers to the next level. Jenny addresses us as "smart, talented, and optimistic." Whether we are actually smart, talented, and optimistic does not matter. Don't we all like to think we aspire to be these things?

This is a great example of a brain-friendly statement that connects on a personal level and even succeeds in complimenting the reader. Jenny has already demonstrated her coaching abilities in her statement by making us come away feeling better even before we have met her.

Many people at one time or another in their lives find themselves looking for a job. Personal brand statements can be used to help define yourself as the right candidate for employers. Let's look at how to accomplish this in the next section.

BRAND STATEMENTS FOR JOB SEARCH

One of the best uses of a well-thought-out brand statement is in the job search to answer the question "Who are you and why should we hire you?"

This question for many is one of the most difficult to answer and one where getting it right is vital to establishing yourself as a top candidate. Thinking about the elements and order of your statement to strengthen your position, skills, abilities, and values to match with that of the employers, helps to give you a "brand" they want to hire.

According to Harvard Professors Amy Cuddy and Princeton Psychologist Susan Riske worldwide there are two factors that people judge you on: if you are friendly, well-intentioned, and competent (can you deliver what you promise)?

People that are both friendly and competent are perceived by the brain to not be a threat and we are inclined to help them. People who demonstrate the opposite are people we respond contemptuously towards. Surprisingly those who are a mix, warm but not competent, elicit feelings of pity, while those who are perceived as competent but not warm provoke envy.

Psychologist Nicolas Kervyn found that when people were presented with facts about two groups of people, one warm and one cold, the participants tended to assume that the warm group was less competent than the cold group. Likewise, if participants knew one group to be competent and the other not, they asked questions whose answers confirmed their hunch that the first group was cold and the second warm. The upshot? "Your gain on one [trait] can be your loss on the other," says Kervyn.

Balancing competence and warmth are vital to projecting the right perception. A long list of accomplishments in past jobs, or in school, may heighten your perception as being competent, but it will not support the idea that you are friendly. The opposite is also true. If you only talk about how you want to save the planet, work selflessly for the betterment of humankind, or the only thing that matters is your family, you may score high on the warm and friendly scale, but people will question your abilities.

51

Let's take a look at a few brand statement examples starting with those from people searching for jobs.

EXAMPLES OF JOB SEARCH BRAND STATEMENTS

Example statements are from actual people who have used the brand tool. To protect their privacy, we do not disclose names.

1. I am an ambitious, sympathetic and fun person who believes in excellence and working together as a diverse team to achieve the common goals. I am known for my curious approach and accuracy in completing my tasks. I strive to be a warm person and active listener who my customers and co-workers can depend on.

2. I endeavor to have a servant's heart who puts himself in the line of fire to enable my co-workers to achieve their best. Exemplary customer service is my unique passion, and exceeding customer expectations is my goal.

3. I am an enthusiastic software engineer that aspires to be reliable and productive in my work. I am known for my good sense of humor and use that to connect with my co-workers. I value open communication, dependability, and openness in others and set this as a standard for myself. I look

for new ways to challenge myself, and desire to work with others I can learn from.

4. I am warm-hearted and considerate and work hard to win the respect of others. I believe respect is the key to getting the best out of people. I am committed to achieving goals through the creation of a common understanding. I work hard to exceed expectations and am always open to new challenges.

5. I am an enthusiastic and dependable problem-solving leader who seeks to deliver the best solutions through collaboration and teamwork. I am known for my thoughtful and out of the box approach, which invites an open flow of ideas and communication. I am open-minded, curious, flexible, and fair in my work relations with others. I deeply value integrity and believe it leads to trusting relationships. When the team is focused, and customers are made a priority, success follows.

The above statements are all diverse in what they say, but what they share are the elements of friendliness and competency.

Let's look at the first statement, from a social media marketing professional, Karla (not her real name) as an example.

53

(1) I am an ambitious, sympathetic and fun person who believes in excellence and working together in a diverse team to achieve the common goals of a company. (2) I am known for my curious approach and accuracy in completing my tasks. (3) I strive to be a warm person and active listener who my customers and co-workers can depend on.

The elements of friendliness are in the 1st and 3rd sentences. In the first statement, Karla expresses she is sympathetic and fun, two qualities that people admire in others and like to work alongside. In the 3rd sentence, she again communicates her friendliness using the word warm. The word warm triggers in our brain a nice feeling, so it is an excellent choice of words here.

The elements of competency are also firmly rooted in this statement. Karla states she believes in excellence and is accurate in completing tasks. To employers this is important. They want people who strive for quality and are conscientious in their work. She ends with a powerful statement, which I think is something that makes her stand out, stating that she is an active listener who co-workers and customers can depend on. Being dependable is also something that all employers look for, but what makes this statement stronger is that Karla connects this to those she works with and to customers. By placing customers in this statement, she makes it clear she understands the importance of customers to business success. It is a brilliant last statement.

The other example statements also strike a good balance between friendliness and competency. When you write your brand statement, you should take a moment to consider whether you have achieved the correct balance. Ask friends, family, job counselors, advisors, and others whose opinions you trust to read it. Ask them if they see both elements of warmth and competency in your statement.

One thing to try with people is to let them read your brand statement and then ask them to tell 4 things about you. Write down the 4 things they said, and then see if there is a balance between the friendly person and the qualified person.

Next, we will look at statements you can use for expressing how you lead and work in teams.

LEADERSHIP BRAND STATEMENT

The brand statement is important for leaders within organizations. In my 15 years of developing leaders in multinational companies, it has become clear that having a leadership brand statement can go a long way towards leading more effectively.

Zenger and Folkman researched 51,836 leaders around the world and found two factors that determine if a person is perceived as being a good leader: warmth and competence. That's right, it is the same two that the Harvard researchers found that people judge one another on. Leaders need to understand that the title of "boss" doesn't automatically bring respect, trust or belief in your abilities. Those are things that must be actively cultivated and nurtured every day.

Just as it is essential to show your ability to do the job by taking on challenging projects, or solving business problems, it is as necessary to be proactive, even strategic, in expressing warmth. Empathy towards those you work with and those you lead is essential to creating your perception as a competent leader who can be trusted.

A well-written personal brand statement gives you the possibility to define how you view others and how you want to work and lead them. It is an opportunity to open the doors to a better conversation with others, and it is through better conversations that we reveal our warmth and reinforce trust.

Let's look at some leadership brand statements as examples.

EXAMPLES OF LEADERSHIP BRAND STATEMENTS

Example statements are from actual people who have used the brand tool. To protect their privacy, we do not disclose names or companies.

1. I'm an open, creative and organized leader. I trust in the power of a good group spirit and look for consensus in decision making. I drive things forward.

2. I am a thoughtful and energetic leader who promotes learning, creativity, and practical teamwork to efficiently achieve goals. I am known for being steady, level-headed, and kind in my decision making. I value close relationships and collaboration along with using knowledge and creativity to lead and motivate a team.

57

3. I am a leader who is always looking for new ways to improve our working methods and processes to help improve the everyday life of others. I have experience from many parts of the company which provides me with an excellent picture of how things are done in the company and how those could be improved. I treat people equally and I am always open to new ideas. I value learning through challenges. Challenges are opportunities to re-evaluate our current state and see if there is room for improvements.

4. I am a reliable, committed and a thoughtful leader who believes in helping our customers find solutions to improve their operations. I am known for following tasks through to completion and developing excellent customer relationships. I am open-minded, hardworking, and flexible in my work relations with others. I believe providing high-quality products sets us apart from our competitors. A good team spirit is vital to our success.

5. I am a logical, analytic, and team-oriented person who values independence and creative thinking. I am flexible in my approach to how the team meets its goals and considerate of new ideas and ways of working. I value accountability and believe setting measurable baselines and targets before work has begun will lead to the most significant success.

58

6. Experienced program manager with proven success in deploying IT solutions to enable transformations at leading global companies in challenging environments. Proficient at collaborating across boundaries in a distributed matrix organization to secure end-to-end execution. Known for having a highly structured approach and perseverance in delivering solutions to clients.

7.

What do these statements have in common? They all express – with authenticity – what the author values and how they like to work. But you can see each is unique in what they reveal about the leader.

Each statement helps to open the conversation on how to work better with that individual. Take for example the first brand, the individual values creativity but only when organized. There is a subtle but important difference between saying "I value creativity" and "I value creativity and organization." Can you spot the difference?

For this person, creativity needs to be controlled. Some might argue that this is not pure creativity but knowing this about the

59

person helps you understand how to work with them. They are open to new ideas, but you must present them in a well-planned way.

Let's look at another example. The person in statement 4 is customer-focused. They look for solutions that best support the customer. Every statement in this brand is about the customer and how the work they do helps them. When working with this individual, it would be important to keep this high level of customer focus into consideration. What could you do to support better customer service and fulfillment of customer needs?

Can you see how valuable your statement can be in a leadership situation? We all have heard of and used "user manuals." A user manual is a document that tells you how to use a machine, or piece of software. What if every person came with a user manual? Think of how much more we could accomplish together.

If you think of your brand as a user manual about how to work with me, you will put your mind into the right state when you begin to formulate your statement.

Let's go back to warmth as a leadership quality. When you take the time to express what is important to you in working with others, you demonstrate you care about them and you want to succeed together. Have you ever worked with someone and found it very difficult to understand what they want and what is driving them? Help others get that understanding of you, and you will forever change how they look and interact with you.

EXPERT/TEAM LEADER BRAND STATEMENTS

Example statements are from actual people who have used the brand tool. To protect their privacy, we do not disclose names or companies.

When writing a brand statement for working with others, you should consider the different dynamic of leading, but not supervising.

Let's look at some examples of these types of brand statements.

1. I am a resourceful expert in my field who believes in helping my co-workers and clients achieve their goals. I am known for my humor and compassion which provides comfort and promotes trust. I own my challenges and failures

61

and will take accountability for my work, my product and my team. I value imagination, resourcefulness, and trust and I believe these are the values of successful leaders. I revel in being a dependable problem solver for my group and my clients.

2. I am an experienced, technical thinker who can work across multiple disciplines and can spot and promote synergy among my colleagues in and out of my immediate organization. I can communicate technical concepts to individuals outside the specialized domains in which I work. At the same time, I can translate the interests of such people into the technical terms often required for significant advances. This often leads to innovative solutions to the most troublesome problems. My goal is to recognize the interests and abilities of my peers (internal and external) and to promote them. Inclusiveness is a priority for me, and I work to expose talent across the organization.

3. I am energetic, reliable, and focused on the team's goals and objectives. I am known for being honest and direct and try to lead by example. I enjoy collaboration and value other people's perspectives and knowledge. I deeply value communication, openness, and honesty and believe these are essential to a team's potential.

I'm customer-focused and always looking for ways to improve myself.

4.   I am an experienced software engineer who loves solving challenging problems that require creativity and application of new skills and knowledge. I have a proven track record planning and leading the successful development of new products on tight timelines and budgets, often despite ambiguous requirements and unanswered technical questions. I take great pride in my work and am not satisfied until I have shipped robust code that will serve as a steady foundation for future development.

5.   I'm interested in learning and development of new things. I want to find out new ways to work and collaborate with others. I like challenges and problem-solving. I value accountability and collaboration. A positive mindset is important to me and change should be an opportunity for development.

Dissecting these brands, we can see the tone is less direct. There is a difference in the relationship dynamics when you are not supervising a person. In these situations, it is important to express your ability to work with others well and what you bring that will help others to be successful.

Let's consider the first statement, from George (not his real name), a young technical engineer. The author has highlighted several important aspects that highlight how he is valuable to the team. Let's break down his statement.

I am a resourceful expert in my field (2) who believes in helping my co-workers and clients achieve their goals. (3) I am known for my humor and compassion which provides comfort and promotes trust. (4) I own my challenges and failures and will take accountability for my work, my product and my team.

The first sentence (1) tells the reader he is a qualified expert in his field. This information is important for creating credibility and for showing the qualifications necessary to do the job. People must be able to trust in your ability to complete the job.

Next, is the statement that George believes it is important to help his co-workers and clients achieve their goals (2). He is committed to the success of others and works to assist his co-workers and clients in the achievement of their goals. We all want to believe our co-workers are devoted to mutual success. Being customer-focused is also extremely important to those you work with.

Without customers none of us have a job. Affirming your focus on customers demonstrates to others you value customer success.

I always tell people I coach, those you work with want to know they are working with a human being and not a robot. In the third part (3), George is humanizing himself by describing a quality that people admire – his humor. We all like to work with people who are fun and have a good sense of humor. By stating that he has this quality and compassion, we get a strong sense he would be someone we would enjoy working with.

Lastly, George states his ability to own challenges and be accountable (4). A strong statement that hits at the heart of working well. Customers and companies want people who own up to their responsibilities and can be trusted not to shift blame to others.

George's statement is a brand that hits all the right areas for working with others. When you read it, you can feel your system 1 lizard brain telling you that this is a solid and competent person that would be enjoyable to work with.

USING THE BRANDING TOOL

PART ONE: THE SURVEY

Visit https://createmybrand.us to get registered to take the survey and get your personalized workbook that goes along with this section.

The branding tool is divided into two parts. The first part is a brief questionnaire that asks you to identify aspects of your personality, your strengths, challenges, and values. It is designed to help you think about yourself by asking questions to get to the core of who you are as a person.

Some of you may have taken personality or behavior assessments in the past, tools like the Myers-Briggs Type Indicator or the DISC behavior assessment. Our tool shares elements of those assessments, but its purpose is different. Its goal is not for clinical or psychological evaluation but for helping you to craft the ideal perception of *you*.

Perception is the key word to remember. The information you get from a psychological assessment is of no importance when you are looking for a job or seek to establish better relationships with those you work. It only reveals who you are, its purpose is not to help you form the perception in others of who you want to be. Let me explain...

It is within your power to shape others' perception of you. Your darkest personality traits do not, and should not, be a part of this perception. We all have areas of ourselves we do not wish to share with others, and it is okay not to share them. What we want to share are the things about us that help others to understand the positive aspects of who we are.

Let's look at the purpose of the branding tool through the eyes of the Johari Window. The Johari Window was developed by psychologist Joseph Luft and Harrington Ingham to help people understand the relationships between themselves and others. It divides the self into 4 quadrants. The first is the **Open** quadrant, which includes the things everyone knows about you and you know about yourself. Things as simple as your sex, your age, your education, how tall you are, hair color, if you are married or single, etc.

The second quadrant comprises **Hidden** things, those things you know about yourself, but others do not see. We all have things we know about ourselves but do not feel comfortable sharing with others. It might be an insecurity or something we are embarrassed to admit. It is okay to have this **Hidden** area; everyone has one and it is normal and healthy.

The third quadrant is the **Blind Spot** and this comprises things others know about us, but we don't know about ourselves. We have all met people who have something about them that is holding them back, or not helping them to be successful and are just not aware of it. This is known as the **Blind Spot**.

The last quadrant is the **Unconscious**. This is an area we don't know about ourselves – things others also don't know. This area is only opened by professional counseling and is not part of our work here.

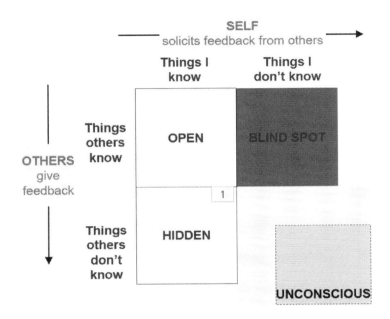

What is the goal here? The goal is to reduce the Hidden quadrant and the Blind Spot.

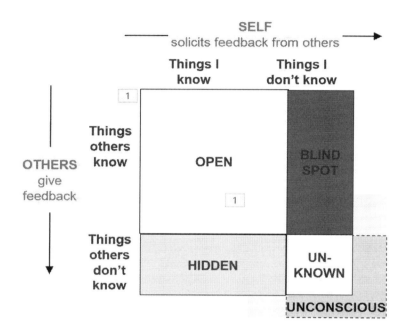

The brand tool can open the **Hidden** quadrant and possibly even the **Blind Spot** by helping you to take an honest look at yourself and what is important to you.

The questions in the first part of the tool, the survey part, are designed to help you explore the perception you have of yourself. When you take the survey, it's not important whether the opinion you have of yourself is 100% accurate or if others share the same perception. It is best to answer the survey with complete honesty.

In part two we will take you step-by-step through the process of examining your results and determine if what you have chosen supports you in building a favorable perception – a perception others find persuasive.

PART TWO OF THE BRAND TOOL: THE WORKSHEET

Get your own personalized worksheet by visiting https://createmybrand.us/ and taking the survey. You will be emailed directly your results and the worksheet to complete.

The second part of the brand tool is the brand worksheet. Its purpose is to take you step-by-step through your answers from part one and guide you through the process of analyzing your perceptions.

WHAT KIND OF PERSON ARE YOU?

Jeff Bezos, the founder of Amazon, is credited with saying "Your brand is what other people say about you when you're not in the room." What people say can be expressed by the formula:

Strengths + Talents +/- Behaviours = Value to those you serve

S + T + B = V

BEHAVIORS CAN, AND OFTEN ARE, A NEGATIVE QUANTITY THAT CAN INVERSELY AFFECT YOUR PERCEIVED VALUE.

The first part of the worksheet looks at how you think others perceive you. The survey asked you to pick one of four types as the one you believe have the characteristics that people would use to describe you.

This part of the survey is based on William Moulton Marston's DISC behavior assessment. DISC is a widely used assessment for helping determine your behavioral style. Some people like to refer to it as your personality, but technically your personality is a bit more complicated. But the types Marston developed are useful in describing your dominant personal behavior type.

The four types are (1) Dominance, (2) Influencer, (3) Steadiness and (4) Compliance (DISC). The numbers 1 to 4 represent the types in our survey and the worksheet results. You were asked to pick one as representing how you believe most people perceive you. Your choice is recorded in the "Your choice" area.

Your choice: TWO Enthusiastic, Persuasive, Animated, Energetic, Talkative, Spontaneous

Characteristics of the Four Types:

ONE	TWO
Communicate directly and are known as a problem solver. You are organized. You are motivated by challenges. You fear being taken advantage.	You are enthusiastic and emotional. You are highly creative. You need to be liked. You fear being rejected and get annoyed by people who cannot listen.
THREE	FOUR
You are a team player and friendly. You are a good listener. You dislike change. You are motivated by recognition. You fear a loss of security and you try to avoid confrontation.	You are analytical and pessimistic. You base your world on facts and provide analytical feedback to others. You are motivated by high standards and quality. You fear criticism.

The worksheet then provides an overview of all 4 types and asks you to analyze if the one you chose is the one you think genuinely describes you and how you would like others to perceive you.

73

How we are, and how we want people to view us are often two separate things.

Let's say you think people would describe you as a type one **Dominant** but you don't identify with that type. You see it as too hard and direct and you would prefer to be seen as softer and more people focused. Your brand statement could highlight your softer aspects to prime people's brains to look for your softer and not your hard, dominant side.

Priming the brain is a technique that is used by marketers to train your brain to look for specific information. Let me demonstrate how it works by recreating the famous priming experiment by Russian psychologist Alfred Lukyanovich Yarbus conducted in 1967.

Look at the following painting entitled 'The Unexpected Visitor'.

Now hide the image and answer the following question:

How many pictures are on the wall?

Look back at the picture. Were you right? I am sure you got it very wrong. Why? Because your brain was not primed to look for that information. You were primed to look at the people in the painting. The title 'The Unexpected Visitor' primed your brain and focused your eye movements on the people in the room and what they are doing.

Applying this technique to your brand statement you can focus people on the things that you want them to "see" and avoid those that you do not want them to see.

It is important to remember that in many situations, such as in a job search, or joining a new team, people have yet to meet you and have nothing to base their perception on. This means you have a blank page to help direct them towards the perception you want them to have of you.

Some might be concerned that we are being less than truthful with people if we are trying to sell ourselves as something we are not.

76

Although this might be true, you need to remember the goal of your statement. Your brand is meant to express the *ideal you*, what you would like to be, how you would want to work, and what is important to you. It is up to you to live up to that ideal in how you conduct yourself and walk the talk.

You can look on it as an exercise in marketing and presenting yourself as a product in the best possible light. Think if product marketing only told 100% of the truth, would we ever buy anything? Probably not.

Let's take, for example, a chocolate candy bar. It has lots of good and bad qualities and it is up to the marketer to highlight the good qualities and minimize the bad ones. To illustrate this point, look at the two examples here. Which one would you buy?

Would you buy the one that is 90% fat-free or the one that has 10% fat? For most, the 90% fat-free is more seductive, and this is how marketers frame their products. Does the candy bar have 10% fat? Yes, it does. But is that what the candy manufacturer wants you as the customer to focus on? No, it is not. Is the glass half-full or half-empty? A good marketer always wants the customer to see the glass as half-full.

Unfortunately, the brain has evolved to see the world as half-empty. Being overly pessimistic helped humans to survive. New situations, ways of doing things, people, were all risks to our survival and the brain evolved to be overly pessimistic. For prehistoric man, taking risks literally got you killed.

It is your job to help people overcome this natural inclination to be pessimistic towards you by framing yourself in a way that focuses them on the positive, on your "90% fat-free."

YOUR IDENTIFIED CHARACTER STRENGTHS

The second part of the survey asks you to identify two signature strengths from a list of six. Research carried out by former

78

President of the American Psychological Association Martin Seligman and University of Michigan Professor Christopher Peterson, and published in the book Character Strengths and Virtues, provides insight into the concept of strengths. Their research confirms each of us has our own signature strengths. Those strengths are broken down and defined as the following:

1. **Wisdom and Knowledge:** creativity, curiosity, open-mindedness, love of learning, perspective, and innovation.

2. **Courage:** bravery, persistence, integrity, vitality, and zest.

3. **Humanity:** love, kindness, social intelligence

4. **Justice:** citizenship, fairness, leadership.

5. **Temperance:** forgiveness and mercy, humility, prudence, and self-control.

6. **Transcendence:** appreciation of beauty and excellence, gratitude, hope, humor, and spirituality.

The worksheet provides your results with the two strengths you chose for yourself, in this format:

79

ONE - Creativity, Curiosity, Open-Mindedness, love of learning, providing wise learning to others

TWO - Bravery, persistence, integrity, approaching life with excitement and energy

I ask you to then verbalize into a single statement how your strengths define you as a person.

POSSIBLE DERAILERS (BLIND SPOTS) TO YOUR POSITIVE BRAND PERCEPTION

The third part of the worksheet looks at the things that could hold you back. I have included this for two reasons. Firstly, it is essential to be honest with yourself about things that might stand in the way of your success. The second is for you to learn how to answer questions that inevitably come up about what you need to improve in yourself or what you find challenging in interview situations. This section gives you insight into those areas and offers an opportunity to reflect on what you can do to overcome them. I ask you to identify from a list 3 things. The results look like this:

You identified 3 things that you find challenging. Those three things are listed here:

Let go and trust others with important tasks, keep my emotions in check when in stressful situations, listen to others when the way forward is so clear.

YOUR PERSONAL VALUES

Finally, I ask about your values. Values form the foundation of your personal truth. Knowing what we value helps us to make decisions and act to fulfill the life we want to live. If you know your values, it becomes easier to pick the correct direction. By helping others to understand your values, you can provide insight to them in how and why they should work with you.

In the survey, I provided a list of values to select from. I did not limit the number you could select but left it open to those that speak to you.

The results are presented like this on the worksheet:

You identified the following values as ones that you have a personal connection to:

Accomplishment, Creativity, Dependability, Diversity, Enthusiasm, Fairness, Growth, Impact, Optimism

The worksheet then asks you to prioritize those values and explain how they are important to you. I also ask you to think if those values would be known to those you work with. Would others be surprised to hear of your values, and why?

CRAFTING YOUR AUTHENTIC PERSONAL BRAND STATEMENT

The last part of the worksheet is to create, or craft, your personal brand statement. I hope, at this point, you have a clearer understanding of yourself and what is important to you.

The challenge now is to put everything together in a statement of around 75 words.

As a good starting point, I suggest that you divide your statement into four parts.

(1) Statement of who you are

(2) What you offer

(3) How your strengths help you achieve success

(4) What you value and how that contributes to making you and those you work with more successful

Let's examine the example from the worksheet to help you understand how to do this. The following is my personal brand statement and comes in at 75 words. The statement was built according to the survey results; my results are recorded above as the examples for each section.

My brand

(1) I am a creative, energetic, and persuasive person who believes in helping people and organizations to achieve more than they thought possible. (2) I am known for my innovative approaches which provide valuable insight and direction. (3) I am open-minded, fair, and flexible in my work relations. (4) I value diversity in all its forms and believe it is the path to greatness. Developing people is my passion. Coaching is a skill. Customers are my priority.

Go back and read my statement again in its entirety. Now imagine that you're thinking of hiring me for a job to help train and develop people.

83

Now do one quick exercise: turn over the paper and write three things you know about me. When you are done, continue below.

What did you come up with? What words immediately came to mind about me? Did they match the core ideas in my brand statement? Was it easy to think of three things?

What feelings did you get when reading it? Did you feel I am a person you would like to work with? Did you get a warm and genuine sense I care for other people? Did I sound sincere in describing myself? Did your lizard brain relax and say, "maybe this guy could help me?" Did your system 2 brain think I have skills that would be useful in developing people?

I hope you got at least some of these feelings when reading this statement. I am not saying it is perfect and you would get these feelings, but I hope at least a few of them. I hope that my genuine desire to help people achieve came across strong and that you can identify a couple of my abilities.

Let's examine in depth my statement and see how I constructed it.

In the first sentence, I set out to accomplish 3 things:

1. Appease the system 1 lizard brain – show I am not a threat: "I help people"
2. Appease the system 2 brain by giving my key competencies: "I am creative, energetic, and persuasive"
3. Provide my competitive advantage: "I am a person who believes in helping people and organizations to achieve more than they thought possible"

In the second sentence, I work to reinforce my competencies and why they are useful to others: "I am known for my innovative approaches which provide valuable insight and direction."

The third and fourth sentences are also focused on the system 1 lizard brain. These sentences help the reader to understand that I am a person that respects people: "I am open-minded, fair, and flexible in my work relations. I value diversity in all its forms and believe it is the path to greatness."

Finally, I connect my values and use it to summarize myself, and what I believe: "Developing people is my passion. Coaching is a skill. Customers are my priority."

I will admit that my statement took many revisions before I was happy with it. When you write your brand, it is good to do the first draft and then put it aside. It might even be best to leave it overnight. Then come back to it with fresh eyes and see does it have the message you want it to have.

Your statement also needs to evolve as you evolve as a person; it should be a living document. Revisit your statement every six months and adjust.

CONCLUSIONS

To quote <u>William Bernbach</u>, one of the original Mad Men:

Nothing is so powerful as an insight into human nature... what compulsions drive a man, what instincts dominate his action... if you know these things about a man you can touch him at the core of his being.

I hope that I have opened your mind and provided insight into the process of creating a unique brand statement that will touch people at the core of their being.

We are bombarded by marketing and advertising that seeks to do that. With thought and imagination, you can tap into these techniques to set yourself apart from the sea of competition and take control of others' perceptions of you.

A well-formulated brand statement is the first step you can take to positively influence how others view you. Being able to then express that statement to those you meet and connecting that statement to your values and then to your specific experience, will confirm their perceptions and set you on a path to success.

ACTION VERBS

I have included here a list of action verbs that can help you find the words that fit into your brand statement. It can be a challenge to find the right words to describe your experience. I hope that this list provides a starting point to triggering your mind.

Leadership Skills

achieved	delegated	improved
administered	developed	incorporated
analyzed	directed	increased
appointed	eliminated	initiated
assigned	emphasized	inspected
attained	enforced	instituted
authorized	enhanced	led
chaired	established	managed
considered	evaluated	merged
consolidated	executed	motivated
contracted	expanded	organized
controlled	generated	originated
converted	handled	overhauled
coordinated	headed	oversaw
decided	hired	pioneered
	hosted	planned

89

presided

prioritized

produced

recommended

reduced (losses)

reorganized

replaced

restored

scheduled

secured

selected

streamlined

strengthened

supervised

surpassed

terminated

**Communication/
People Skills**

addressed

advertised

arbitrated

arranged

articulated

authored

clarified

collaborated

communicated

composed

condensed

conferred

contacted

conveyed

convinced

corresponded

debated

defined

described

developed

directed

discussed

drafted

edited

elicited

enlisted

explained

expressed

formulated

furnished

influenced

interacted

interpreted

interviewed

involved

joined

judged

lectured

listened

marketed

mediated

moderated

negotiated

observed

outlined

participated

persuaded

presented

promoted

proposed

publicized

reconciled

recruited

referred

reinforced

reported

resolved

responded

solicited

specified

spoke

suggested

summarized

synthesized

translated

wrote

Problem-Solving

Skills

analyzed

clarified

collected

compared

conducted

critiqued

detected

determined

diagnosed

evaluated

examined

experimented

explored

extracted

formulated

gathered

identified

interpreted

invented

investigated

located

measured

organized

researched

reviewed

searched

solved

summarized

surveyed

tested

Technical Skills

adapted

applied

assembled

built

calculated

computed

conserved

constructed

converted

debugged

designed

determined

developed

engineered

fortified

installed

maintained

operated

overhauled

printed

programmed

91

rectified

regulated

remodeled

repaired

replaced

restored

solved

specialized

spearheaded

standardized

studied

upgraded

utilized

Teaching Skills

adapted

advised

clarified

coached

communicated

conducted

coordinated

critiqued

developed

enabled

encouraged

evaluated

explained

facilitated

focused

guided

informed

instilled

instructed

motivated

persuaded

set goals

simulated

stimulated

taught

tested

trained

transmitted

tutored

Financial/

Data Skills

administered

adjusted

allocated

analyzed

appraised

assessed

audited

balanced

budgeted

calculated

computed

conserved

corrected

determined

developed

estimated

forecasted

managed

marketed

measured

planned

prepared

programmed

projected

92

reconciled

reduced

researched

retrieved

saved

Creative Skills

acted

adapted

began

combined

composed

conceptualized

condensed

created

customized

designed

developed

directed

displayed

drew

edited

entertained

established

fashioned

formulated

founded

illustrated

initiated

instituted

integrated

introduced

invented

modeled

modified

originated

performed

photographed

planned

revised

revitalized

shaped

solved

wrote

Counseling Skills

adapted

advocated

assessed

assisted

cared for

clarified

coached

counseled

demonstrated

diagnosed

educated

encouraged

ensured

expedited

facilitated

familiarized

furthered

guided

intervened

mediated

mentored

motivated

prevented

provided

referred

93

rehabilitated

represented

resolved

simplified

supported

Organization/Detail Skills

approved

arranged

catalogued

categorized

charted

classified

coded

collected

compiled

corrected

corresponded

distributed

executed

filed

generated

implemented

incorporated

indexed

inspected

inventoried

logged

maintained

monitored

obtained

operated

ordered

organized

prepared

processed

provided

purchased

recorded

registered

reserved

responded

retrieved

reviewed

routed

scheduled

screened

set up

submitted

supplied

standardized

systematized

updated

validated

verified

Development Skills

analyzed

applied

catalogued

compiled

conceived

created

designed

developed

established

formulated

founded

influenced

94

implemented	administered	achieved
initiated	approved	completed
instituted	arranged	expanded
supported	coordinated	exceeded
surveyed	designed	improved
tabulated	established	pioneered
updated	evaluated	reduced (losses)
Time-	headed	resolved (issues)
Management	hired	restored
Skills	interpreted	spearheaded
administered	interviewed	succeeded
developed	managed	surpassed
directed	mediated	transformed
generated	negotiated	won
improved	organized	
initiated	prepared	
increased	planned	
promoted	supervised	
reduced	**Additional Verbs**	
Administrative	**for**	
Skills	**Accomplishments**	

ADDITIONAL READING

Simone Kühn , Jürgen Gallinat, *Does Taste Matter? How Anticipation of Cola Brands Influences Gustatory Processing in the Brain* http://journals.plos.org/plosone/article?id=10.1371/journal.pone.0061569

Read Montague, *Coke or Pepsi? It's all in the head* https://www.theguardian.com/world/2004/jul/29/science.research

Thinking Fast and Slow by Daniel Kahneman: https://en.wikipedia.org/wiki/Thinking,_Fast_and_Slow

2013 study done by Hannah Gacey and Jim Gallo - *Some SCIENCE Behind the Smiley… Emoticons and Their Possible Impact on the Workplace:* http://www.hrfloridareview.org/item/266-some-science-behind-the-smiley-emoticons-and-their-possible-impact-on-the-workplace

Paul Zak, *How Stories Change the Brain:* https://greatergood.berkeley.edu/article/item/how_stories_change_brain

USC Professor of Neuroscience Antonio Damasio and his work with understanding emotion: https://en.wikipedia.org/wiki/Antonio_Damasio

David Shoorman, Interpersonal trust: http://www.krannert.purdue.edu/directory/bio.php?username=schoor

Amy Cuddy and Princeton Psychologist Susan Riske, *Mixed Impressions: How We Judge Others on Multiple Levels:* https://www.scientificamerican.com/article/mixed-impressions/

Nicolas Kervyn, *Competence and warmth in context: The compensatory nature of stereotypic views of national groups.* http://nicolaskervyn.blogspot.com/

Zenger and Folkman, *I'm the Boss! Why Should I Care If You Like Me?* https://hbr.org/2013/05/im-the-boss-why-should-i-care

Joseph Luft and Harrington Ingham, The Johari Window https://en.wikipedia.org/wiki/Johari_window

Christopher Pertersen and Martin Seligman, *Character Strengths and Virtues* https://en.wikipedia.org/wiki/Character_Strengths_and_Virtues

William Bernbach, The original Mad Man of Advertising https://en.wikipedia.org/wiki/William_Bernbach

RESOURCES

All resources are freely available at the time of publication.

Take the accompanying survey to help you understand yourself better and get the personal workbook to assist in writing your brand statement: http://www.createmybrand.us

Check the readability of your statement – it is good to strike a balance between being easily understood (i.e. a lower-grade level) and intelligent (a higher-grade level). Depending on your audience adjust accordingly. https://www.webpagefx.com/tools/read-able/

Check the tone of your statement using IBM's Watson   supercomputer: https://tone-analyzer-demo.ng.bluemix.net/

Explore deeper your strengths and take the Via Institute on Character's free Strength Survey: https://www.viacharacter.org/

Understand your dominate personality type: Take the   online   DISC   assessment: https://www.123test.com/disc-personality-test/

The Elevator Pitch of You

Made in the USA
Las Vegas, NV
18 May 2021

23234157R00058